MONSTER MATH
Puzzles and Games
WORKBOOK

Ages 6 to 8

By Martha Cheney
Illustrated by Yvonne Cherbak

Lowell House
Juvenile
Los Angeles

CONTEMPORARY BOOKS
Chicago

Reviewed and endorsed by Ronn Yablun, author of **Mathamazement** and **How to Develop Your Child's Gifts and Talents in Math**.

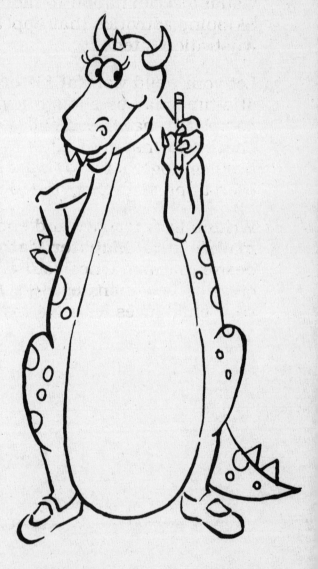

Lowell House Books can be purchased at special discounts when ordered in bulk for premiums and special sales. Contact Department JH at the following address:

Lowell House Juvenile
2020 Avenue of the Stars, Suite 300
Los Angeles, CA 90067

ISBN: 1-56565-518-4

Manufactured in the United States of America

10 9 8 7 6 5 4 3 2

Note to Parents

With a team of creative monster instructors, **Monster Math** is a wonderful learning tool that will give your child a head start in math. The cognitive and deductive skills learned will create a solid foundation in analytical thinking that your child can build upon with continued education.

The activities in this book contain a range of difficulty levels, from basic addition and subtraction to beginning multiplication, division, and fractions. It is important that your child complete the activities in order, since the book progresses from simple visual discrimination to more advanced problem solving. Skipping activities that appear early in the book may cause frustration later.

Let your child work at his or her own pace—four or five pages at a time may be enough for one sitting. After each activity is completed, have your child turn to the back of the book to check the answer(s). If an answer is incorrect, review the problem together and make sure your child understands everything before moving to the next activity.

Written by a teacher and endorsed by a professor of mathematics, **Monster Math** will benefit any child who has a desire to learn. Once your child has completed the book, try creating new monster story problems to solve. You may find your child loves learning math—and has the skills to prove it!

RIMSLEY'S RIDDLES

Rimsley has drawn four figures. He has written a description of each figure in the form of a riddle. Draw a line from each figure to the description that matches it.

I am made of three squares.
None of the squares are the same size.

I am made of triangles and circles.
My triangles are all inside my circles.

I contain a rectangle, a triangle, and a circle.
There is a small square in my middle.

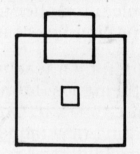

I am made of three different shapes.
None of my shapes touch each other.

SOME RIDDLES OF YOUR OWN

Look at the figures Rimsley has drawn on this page for you. Write your own riddles to go with each figure.

1.

_____
_____
_____
_____

2.

_____
_____
_____
_____

3.

_____
_____
_____
_____

THE MISSING PIECE

Ursula and Millie are working on a jigsaw puzzle. Look at the picture below. Which of the remaining pieces will finish the puzzle? Draw a circle around it.

SILLY SUBTRACTION

Jag and Milo are playing a game and they want you to play, too! Jag draws a figure. Milo erases part of the figure. You must draw the part of the figure that is left. The first one is done for you.

Jag drew: Milo erased: What is left?

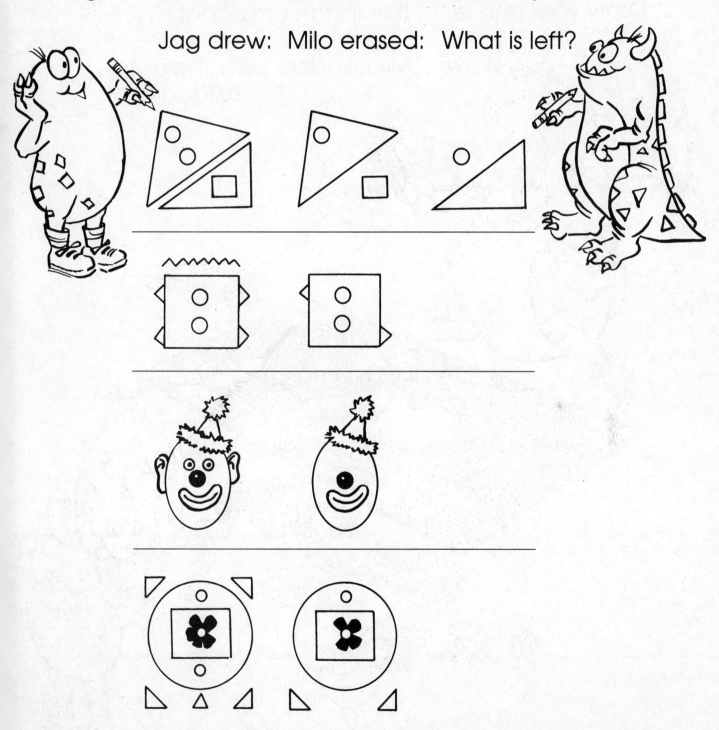

DAFFY ADDITION

This time instead of erasing part of Jag's figure, Milo has decided he's going to add something to it. Take a look at each figure. What did Milo add? Draw your answer in the space provided.

Jag drew: Milo added: What was added?

8

A MONSTER PIE

Samantha, Maggie, and Suji want to make an apple pie. Their cookbook says to use 6 apples. According to the recipe, there must be at least 1 red apple and at least 1 green apple in the pie. Color the apples to show the different combinations of red and green apples that the girls might use.

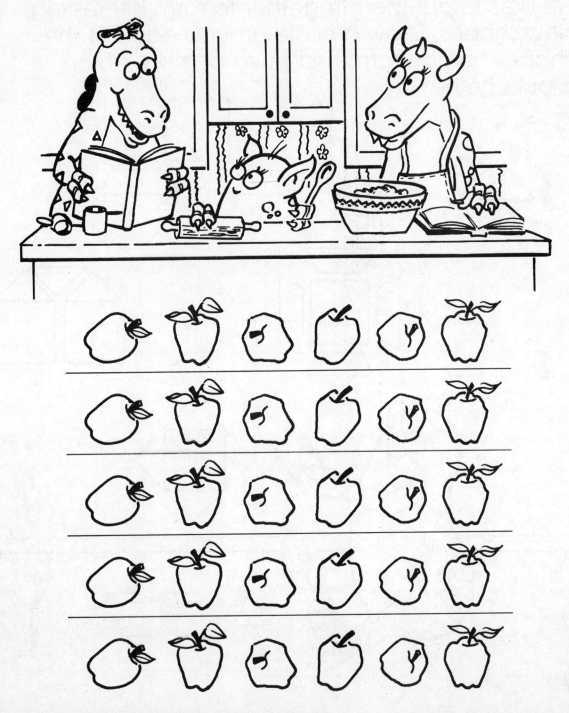

JAG'S PATTERN BLOCKS

Jag has pattern blocks in the following shapes:

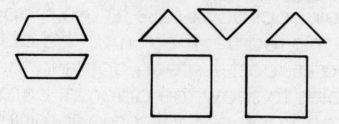

He likes to put them together to form interesting new shapes. Draw a circle around each of the shapes he can form using two or more of the blocks he has.

Now draw some other shapes Jag could form using his blocks.

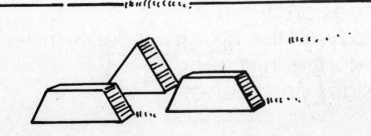

NUMBER CROSSWORD

Jed found this crossword puzzle in the local newspaper, *The Daily Monster*. He needs you to help him fill it in. Read the clues below that describe each number. Write each answer in the puzzle, putting one letter in each box. Be sure to begin each answer in the box that has the same number as the written clue.

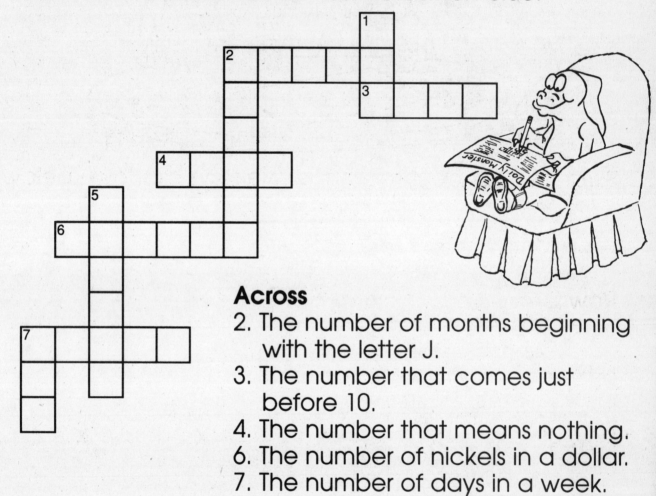

Across
2. The number of months beginning with the letter J.
3. The number that comes just before 10.
4. The number that means nothing.
6. The number of nickels in a dollar.
7. The number of days in a week.

Down
1. The number of toes on two feet.
2. The number of days in the month of September.
5. The number of months in a year.
7. The number of sides on a cube.

JED'S GAME

To play Jed's game you will need a friend and 15 counters. Your counters can be such items as buttons, pennies, or dried beans.

Arrange your counters in the five rows as shown below:

Row 1   X

Row 2   X   X

Row 3   X   X   X

Row 4   X   X   X   X

Row 5   X   X   X   X   X

Each player takes turns picking up counters. On each turn, a player may pick up any or all of the counters **from one row only**. The object is to force your opponent to pick up the last counter.

A MONSTER MIND BENDER

Help Cosmos rearrange each sequence of digits to create the **largest** number possible. Write the number next to its set of digits.

6 4 9 _____

5 8 3 5 _____

6 1 0 8 7 _____

Help Jed rearrange each sequence of digits to make the **smallest** number possible. Write the number next to its set of digits.

8 1 4 _____

7 3 8 2 _____

3 5 6 9 1 _____

HOW MANY WAYS?

Rodney has 3 number cards. Mrs. Murky told him that he can make 6 different 3-digit numbers using his cards. Rodney needs your help to figure out all of the numbers he can make with his cards.

Using only the numbers on the cards Rodney is holding, fill in each set of blank cards to create 5 other different 3-digit numbers.
The first one is done for you.

2 6 7

2 6 7

SCARY SYMMETRY

Suji and Jag are playing a game. Suji draws a scary figure. Jag must draw a line through Suji's figure so that the two sides of the figure look exactly the same. This line is called a **line of symmetry**. Where should he draw the line? Use a ruler to make a straight line and show Jag where the line of symmetry is on each of the figures below. The first one is done for you.

The figures on this page are a little bit trickier. Each figure has 2 different lines of symmetry. Help Jag draw lines through each figure so that he shows both lines of symmetry! Remember to use your ruler so that your lines are straight. The first one is done for you.

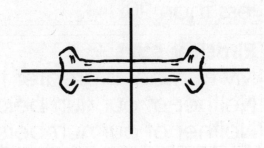

FAVORITE MONSTER NUMBERS

Rimsley and Rodney each have a favorite number.

Rodney says:
My number is **even**. Even numbers can be broken into two equal parts. My number is 2 less than Rimsley's. Our numbers added together equal less than 20.

Rimsley says:
My number is greater than Rodney's. Neither of our numbers is less than 5. Neither of our numbers ends with a 0.

Using the information above, figure out whether each statement below is true or false. Circle your answer.

Rimsley's number is **odd**. Odd numbers cannot be broken into two equal parts.
true   false

Rodney's number is 4.
true   false

Rimsley's number is 6.
true   false

Rodney's number is the same as Rimsley's number.
true   false

The two numbers added together equal 8.
true   false

What are Rodney's and Rimsley's numbers?_____

A CALENDAR CHALLENGE

Samantha just bought a brand-new calendar. She is trying to learn about the days of the week. Can you help her by answering the following questions?

If the day before yesterday was Tuesday, then what day is it today?

_____

What day will it be 1 week from tomorrow?

_____

Samantha's birthday is 9 days away. On which day of the week will her birthday fall?

_____

What day will it be 2 weeks from yesterday?

_____

SUNDAY	MONDAY	TUESDAY	WEDNESDAY	THURSDAY	FRIDAY	SATURDAY
	1	2	3	4	5	6
7	8	9	10	11	12	13
14	15	16	17	18	19	20
21	22	23	24	25	26	27
28	29	30				

MONSTER MONEY

Milo has sorted his coins into three different stacks. He has 8 dimes, 3 quarters, and 20 nickels. Which stack contains the most money? _____

Maggie also has sorted coins into three different stacks. Her stack is much larger that Milo's. **For an extra challenge**, figure out which of Maggie's stacks contains the most money. She has 56 dimes, 22 quarters, and 100 nickels.

PICTURE PROBLEMS

Make up a monster math problem to explain the situation shown in each picture. Here's a sample to get you started.

Problem: If each monster takes 1 toad home for a pet, how many toads will be left?

Answer: **1 toad**

Problem: _____

_____

_____

Answer: _____

Problem: _____

_____

Answer: _____

For an extra challenge, make up additional problems to go along with each picture!

THE MULTIPLIED MONSTER PYRAMID

Fill in the chart at the bottom of the page. The picture of the pyramid will help you!

Number of monsters in the row	1	2	3	4	What if there was a row with 5 monsters?
Eyes					
Spots					
Toes					

URSULA'S GARDEN

Ursula has planted a flower garden. She planned the garden so that the flowers would form a pattern.

To find the pattern:
- Count the petals on each flower.
- Color the flowers with an odd number of petals red. Color the flowers with an even number of petals yellow.

What is Ursula's pattern? _____

Now create your very own flower garden pattern. Give some of the flowers in your garden an even number of petals. Give the other flowers an odd number of petals.

23

MONSTER TALES

Samantha, Suji, Milo, and Jag are at the library. Each monster has checked out a book of monster tales.

Samantha's book has 48 pages. How many of the pages have a 2 in the page number?_____

Suji's book has 64 pages. How many of the pages have a 9 in the page number?_____

Milo's book also has 64 pages. How many of the pages have a 6 in the page number?_____

Jag's book has 32 pages. How many of the pages have a 1 in the page number?_____

NEIGHBORLY NUMBERS

The houses that are on Ursula's street have unusual addresses. Their address numbers are not in numerical order, but they do have something in common. What is it? Write your answer on the lines below.

_____

_____

_____

THE SLIMEPIT COUNTY FAIR

It's the time of year when the monsters go to the county fair. All the monsters love the fair, especially the little ones!

Cosmos likes to play the games the most. In this game he needs 25 points to win the huge stuffed alligator. He gets to roll 5 balls at the target.

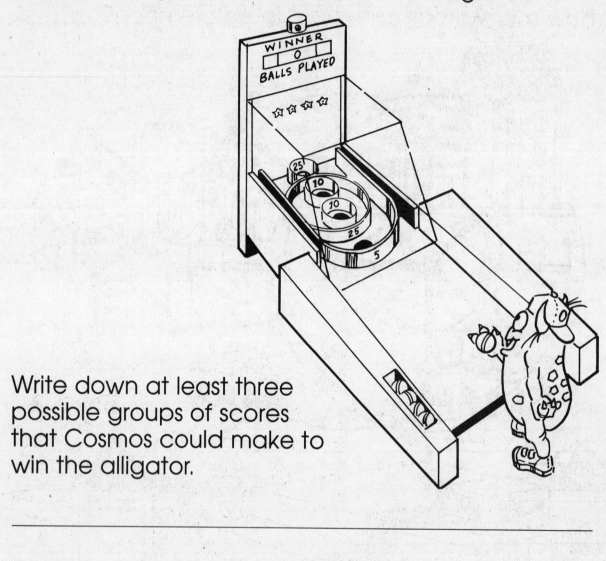

Write down at least three possible groups of scores that Cosmos could make to win the alligator.

_____

_____

_____

Maggie's favorite ride is the Ferris wheel. She loves to ride it over and over again. Each ride lasts 5 minutes. Then it takes 2 minutes to unload the Ferris wheel and 3 minutes for the people who are waiting in line to get on for the next ride.

If Maggie's first ride of the day begins at 11:00 A.M., how many times can she ride before noon? _____

THE GLUBGUT FAMILY

The Glubgut family members all share some common physical traits. Each Glubgut, big or little, has pointed ears and a very large belly. No Glubgut wears glasses or has curly hair.

Circle each member of the Glubgut family.

THE GRUNCHLY FAMILY

The Grunchly family members also have some common physical traits. Each Grunchly has two large front fangs. Each Grunchly has spikes on his or her tail and hairy arms. No Grunchly has furry feet. No Grunchly has a beard, but every Grunchly has a large nose.

How many Grunchly family members can you find on this page? _____

Circle each member.

MAGGIE'S PUZZLE

Maggie has drawn some figures for you to trace with your pencil. She also has made up some challenging rules for you to follow as you trace.

- You may only trace over each line in a figure once.
- You may not pick up your pencil after you have started tracing!

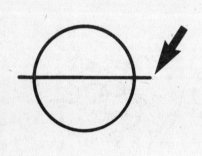

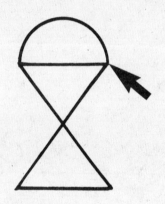

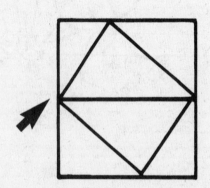

MILO'S PUZZLE

Below is a puzzle that Milo's Grandpa taught him. To solve the puzzle, you must connect the 9 dots by using only 4 straight lines!

Here are two hints to help you:
- Your lines can extend beyond the dots!
- Never keep your brain in a box!

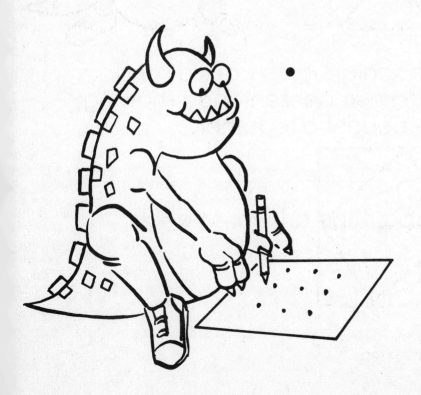

A MONSTER BAKE SALE

Rodney is selling cookies to make money for his Monster Scout Troop. He has both worm chip cookies and bugmeal cookies to sell.

Mrs. Bugle bought 3 of each kind of cookie. Write a number sentence showing how many cookies she bought altogether.

_____ + _____ = _____

Mr. Wobble bought 2 chocolate chip cookies and 4 oatmeal cookies. Write a number sentence showing how many cookies he bought altogether.

_____ + _____ = _____

Mr. Moldy bought 5 chocolate chip cookies and 1 oatmeal cookie. Write a number sentence showing how many cookies he bought altogether.

_____ + _____ = _____

What do you notice about the answer to each number sentence?

_____

_____

NUMBER SENTENCES

Millie wants to match her numbered shape cards to the corresponding shapes in each number sentence. She has to make sure that all of the number sentences make sense. Each of the shape cards can be used only once. Can you help Millie?

MORE NUMBER SENTENCES

Now it's Jag's turn! He wants to match his shape cards to the corresponding shapes in the number sentences. All of the number sentences must make sense. Each of the shape cards can be used only once. Can you help?

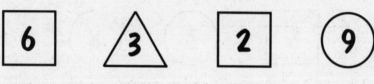

$$\square + \triangle = 14$$

$$\bigcirc + \triangle = 8$$

$$\square + \bigcirc = 13$$

$$\bigcirc + \triangle + \square = 10$$

MONSTER MAGIC

Samantha has some "magic" tricks for your eyes. Look at each picture below carefully and answer the questions.

Which of these lines is longer? Circle that line.

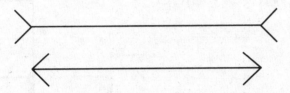

Which monster is taller? Circle that monster.

Are these lines **parallel?** _____ Parallel lines are the same distance apart at all points along the line.

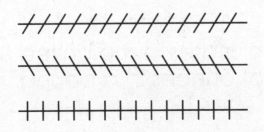

A NUMBER CROSSWORD

Millie loves crossword puzzles, but she needs your help to complete this one. Read the clues below that describe each number. Write each answer in the puzzle, putting one letter in each box. Be sure to begin each answer in the box that has the same number as the written clue.

Across
1. The number of seasons in a year.
3. The number of nickels in a quarter.
4. The number of minutes in an hour.
5. The number of pennies in a dollar: one _____

Down
1. The number of states in the United States.
2. The number of ounces in a pound.
6. Another name for 12.

HEIGHTS AND WEIGHTS

In their health class, the monsters are having their heights and weights measured.

Millie is taller than Suji.
Sam is taller than Millie.
Sam is taller than Suji but shorter than Ursula.

Write the girls' names in order from tallest to shortest.

_____

_____

_____

_____

Jag weighs less than Cosmos.
Jed is heavier than Cosmos.
Rodney is lighter than Jed but heavier than Cosmos.

Write the boys' names in order from heaviest to lightest.

_____

_____

_____

_____

MONSTER MEASUREMENT

People living in the United States use a unit of measurement called a foot to measure length. One foot is 12 inches long, which is about as long as a large human adult foot.

Monsters use a unit of measurement called a monster foot.

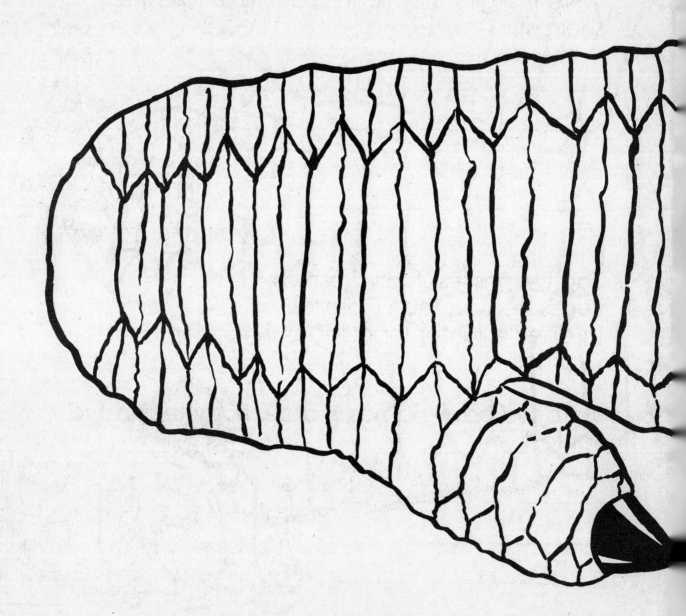

Use a large piece of paper (or tape two sheets together) to trace the monster foot on these two pages. Cut out your monster foot, and use it to answer the questions on the next page.

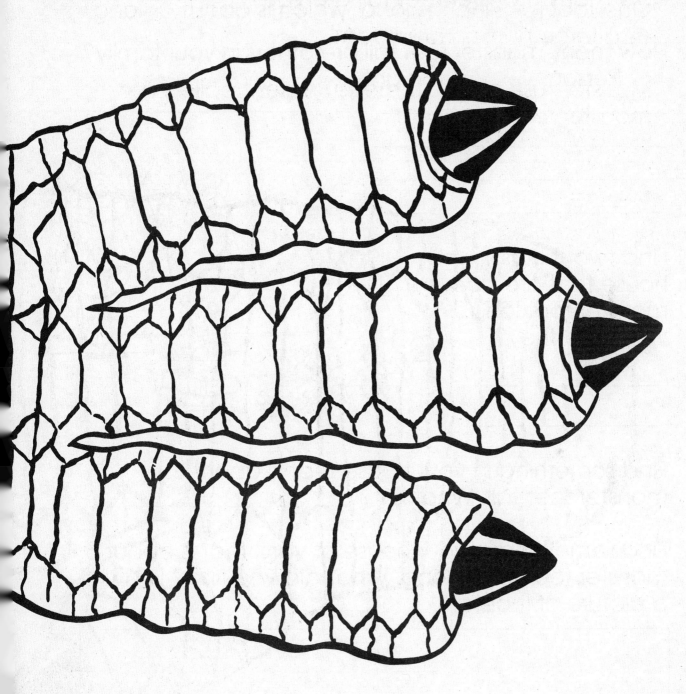

MONSTER MEASUREMENT QUESTIONS

How many monster feet tall are you? _____

How many monster feet tall are others in your family?

Person	Height
_____	_____
_____	_____
_____	_____
_____	_____

Find two things in your house that are about 1 monster foot long. What are they?

_____

_____

Find something in your house that is about 3 monster feet tall. What is it? _____

Find something in your house or yard that is about 5 monster feet tall or long. What did you find? Draw a picture of it below.

PLANNING A PARTY

Millie wants to plan a pizza party for all her friends in September. She needs to be sure that everyone can attend. Millie's friends have written her notes, telling her which days they will not be able to go to the party. Help Millie use the information in the notes to find a date when all her friends will be available.

I can't come to the party on the third Saturday of the month.
Love, Milo

I will be out of town from September 1 to September 11.
Love, Ursula

I can only come to the party on a Friday.
Love, Cosmos

September

SUNDAY	MONDAY	TUESDAY	WEDNESDAY	THURSDAY	FRIDAY	SATURDAY
			1	2	3	4
5	6	7	8	9	10	11
12	13	14	15	16	17	18
19	20	21	22	23	24	25
26	27	28	29	30		

I have to baby-sit on September 24. I could come to the party any other day. Love, Samantha

What is the best date for Millie's party? _____

ZOONIES, GOONIES, AND LOONIES

These are zoonies.

These are goonies.

These are loonies.

Draw a circle around each of the zoonies that you see in the box below. Draw a square around each goonie. Draw a triangle around each loonie.

42

Draw your own zoonie.

Draw your own goonie.

Draw your own loonie.

SUJI'S PUZZLE

Suji made a quilt in the shape of a square. Now she has decided that she wants to make the quilt bigger. She wants it to be twice as large as it is now, but still be in the shape of a square.

How can she do it? Show her by adding onto the picture of the quilt below.

Hint: Suji should add 4 triangles to the quilt.

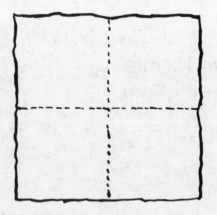

MORE PICTURE PROBLEMS

Make up a monster math problem to explain the situation shown in each picture. Here's a sample to get you started.

Problem: Jed has 6 worms. Millie has 2 more than Jed. How many worms do they have altogether?

Answer: **14 worms**

Problem:_____

_____

_____

Answer:_____

Problem:_____

_____

_____

Answer:_____

For an extra challenge, make up additional problems to go along with each picture!

THE MONSTERS' DAY AT THE BEACH

Rimsley went to the beach with his family. Together, they built a giant sandcastle by packing wet sand into containers of different shapes.

Draw a line from each container to the parts of the sandcastle that were formed by that container.

BUNCHES OF BOXES

Milo is helping his family collect boxes for moving. He has collected 4 big boxes. Inside 2 of these big boxes he has found 3 smaller boxes. Inside the other 2 big boxes there are 2 smaller boxes.

How many boxes does Milo have altogether? Draw the small boxes in the large boxes below. One box is already completed. Count all of the boxes to find the answer.

JAG'S PUZZLE

Jag has been working on math problems all day long. He thinks he has made up a few that are sure to trick you. See if you can figure them out. Remember that **consecutive numbers** are numbers that follow each other in order, like 1, 2, 3 or 57, 58, 59.

Find three consecutive numbers that add up to 15.

_____ _____ _____

Find three consecutive numbers that add up to 45.

_____ _____ _____

Find three consecutive numbers that add up to 75.

_____ _____ _____

What do these answers have in common?

_____

THE MONSTERS HAVE A SPELLING BEE

Five monsters are finalists in the school spelling bee. Use the three clues below to help you find the winner. But be careful! Each clue contains one true and one false statement. Circle the winner.

Clue #1:   The winner is wearing a black vest.
             The winner is smiling.

Clue #2:   The winner is wearing shoes.
             The winner is wearing a white vest.

Clue #3:   The winner is not smiling.
             The winner is not wearing shoes.

A MONSTER BIKE RIDE

Milo went for a bike ride and took a full bottle of water. He stopped to rest twice. The first time he stopped, he drank 1/2 of his water. The next time he stopped, he drank 1/2 of the water that was left. Finish the picture of the water bottle to show how much water was in his bottle when he finished his bike ride.

A LIZARD RACE

To play this game with the monsters, you will need a pair of dice and 12 small markers. These can be items such as dried beans, pennies, or buttons.

Place one marker on each of the 12 lizards in the area marked "START." Notice that each lizard has a number on its back. Now roll the dice. Move the marker for the lizard wearing the number shown on the dice **1** space ahead. Repeat until one marker crosses the finish line.

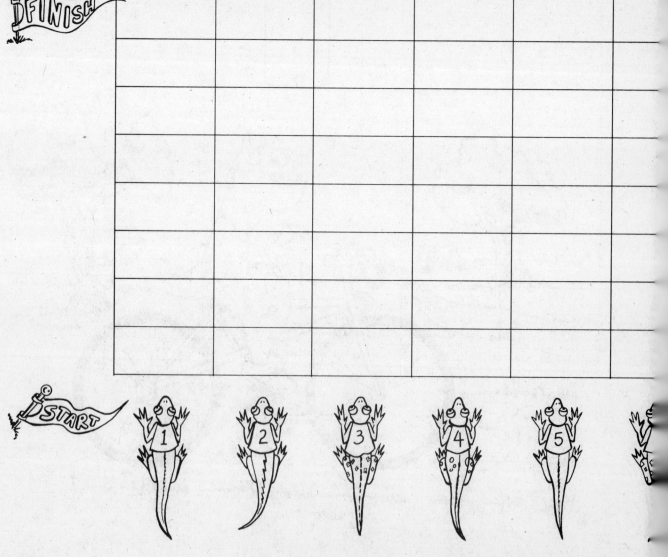

After you have played the game several times, answer these questions.

Can lizard number 1 ever win the race? _____

Why or why not? _____

Which lizards win most often? _____

Why or why not? _____

A SUPER SQUARE

Suji and Jed are trying to figure out the answer to the puzzle below. Each side of the square is made up of four boxes. The numbers in the four boxes on each side must add up to 16. The same number must go in each empty box. Can you help Suji and Jed find the number they need?

ANOTHER SUPER SQUARE

Suji and Jed had so much fun with the first super square that Ursula and Milo have decided to do one. Each side of the square is made up of four boxes. The numbers in the four boxes on each side must add up to 12. The same number must go in each empty box. Can you help Ursula and Milo find the number they need?

	1	7	
6			8
2			0
	3	5	

SAMANTHA'S CIRCLES

Samantha has drawn a set of seven overlapping circles. Each circle must have three numbers that add up to 21. The top circle has been filled in for you. Help Samantha fill in the missing numbers in each of the other circles. You may use the numbers 1 through 14. Use each number only once.

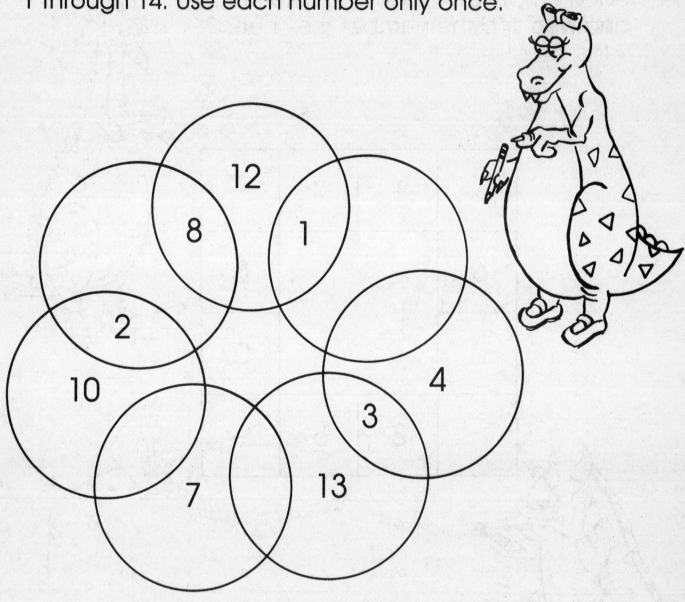

LUNCHTIME

Ursula and Cosmos are sharing their lunches. Together they have 1 sandwich, 2 pickles, 3 cookies, 4 deviled eggs, and 5 carrot sticks. Complete the picture to show one way that they could share the food equally.

Hint: You might need to cut or break some of the food!

SMELLY JELLIES

Cosmos has a big jar of his favorite candies, Smelly Jellies. He wants to know how many Smelly Jellies he has. Use pictures and/or words to explain two different methods Cosmos can use to figure out how many Smelly Jellies he has.

Method 1

Method 2

A GAME OF BASHBALL

Slimepit Elementary is playing Slushpuddle Elementary in a game of bashball. When a monster carries the ball across the goal line, his or her team gets 3 points. When the ball is rolled across the goal line, the team receives 2 points. When the ball is thrown across the goal line, the team scores just 1 point.

Slimepit won the game by a score of 18 to 12. Fill in the tables below with the points scored to show some of the possible combinations of goals made by each team.

Slimepit	Various Possible Scores		
	#1	#2	#3
Carried			
Rolled			
Thrown			
Total	18	18	18

Slushpuddle	Various Possible Scores		
	#1	#2	#3
Carried			
Rolled			
Thrown			
Total	12	12	12

MONSTERS AT THE MOVIES

Milo's little brothers, Mack, Jack, and Flack, went to the movies. They each bought a different treat to enjoy during the film. The monster boys are 6, 7, and 8 years old. Use the clues below to match the ages and treats to the proper monsters.

Mack is older than Jack.
Flack is not the youngest.
The youngest boy likes chocolate bars.
The boy who likes popcorn is the oldest.
Flack does not like licorice.

Name of boy	Age	Favorite Treat
Mack		
Flack		
Jack		

ANSWERS

page 4

I am made of three squares.
None of the squares are the
same size.

I am made of triangles and
circles.
My triangles are all inside my
circles.

I contain a rectangle, a triangle,
and a circle.
There is a small square in my
middle.

I am made of three different
shapes.
None of my shapes touch each
other.

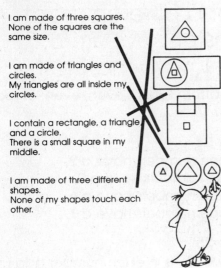

page 5
Answers will vary.

page 6

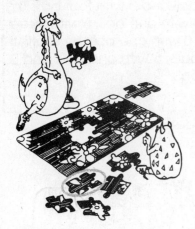

page 7

page 8

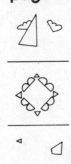

page 9

page 10

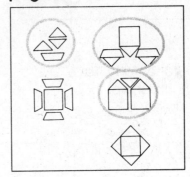

page 11
Answers will vary.

page 12

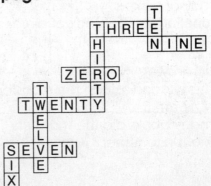

page 13
Answers will vary.

page 14
964   148
8553   2378
87610   13569

page 15
267, 276, 627, 672, 726, 762

page 16

page 17

page 18
false, false, false, false, false
Rodney's number is 6.
Rimsley's number is 8.

page 19
Thursday
Friday
Saturday
Wednesday

page 20
The stack of nickels.
Extra challenge: The stack of dimes.

page 21
Sample answers include:
How many candies can the monster
buy? **Answer:** 5
How many books did the monsters
check out altogether? **Answer:** 7

page 22

Number of monsters in the row	1	2	3	4	What if there was a row with 5 monsters?
Eyes	2	4	6	8	10
Spots	3	6	9	12	15
Toes	4	8	12	16	20

page 23
The pattern is odd, even, even; or red,
yellow, yellow.

page 24
14 page numbers have a 2.
6 page numbers have a 9.
11 page numbers have a 6.
13 page numbers have a 1.

page 25
The two digits in each number add up
to 6.

page 26
Cosmos could score 25 points by scoring
5 points with each ball; by scoring 25
with one ball and 0 with four balls; by
scoring 10 with one ball, 5 with three
balls, and 0 with one ball; by scoring 10
with two balls, 5 with one ball, and 0
with two balls.

page 27
She can ride 6 times.

page 28

page 29
There is one Grunchy on the page.

page 30

Parent: Make sure child traces shapes per instructions on page. The arrows will show them where to start tracing.

page 31

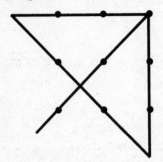

page 32

3 + 3 = 6
2 + 4 = 6
5 + 1 = 6
The answers are all the same.

page 33

1 + 8 = 9
5 + 7 = 12
4 + 9 = 13
2 + 3 + 6 = 11

page 34

6 + 8 = 14
5 + 3 = 8
4 + 9 = 13
1 + 7 + 2 = 10

page 35

The pictures are optical illusions.
Both lines are the same length.
Both monsters are the same height.
The lines are parallel.

page 36

page 37

Ursula, Samantha, Millie, Suji
Jed, Rodney, Cosmos, Jag

pages 38–40

Answers will vary.

page 41

The best date for Millie's party is Friday, September 17.

page 42

page 43

Answers will vary. Zoonies have 3 eyes, 4 squiggly legs, and any closed shape. Goonies are always round. They have 2 straight legs. They can have any expression and any number of eyes. Loonies are always square. They are always smiling. They can have any number of eyes. They have no legs.

page 44

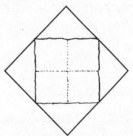

page 45

Sample answers include:
If 2 of the turtles jump into the river, how many little animals will be left with Millie and Jed? **Answer:** 3; 2 snakes and 1 turtle.
How many more fish did Millie catch than Jed? **Answer:** 0. They caught the same number.

pages 46–47

page 48
14 boxes

page 49
4, 5, 6
14, 15, 16
24, 25, 26

They all have 4, 5, and 6 in them.

page 50
The winning monster is wearing the black vest and shoes, but is not smiling. Each monster about whom both statements in a clue is true cannot be the winner, since one of each of the pairs of statements is false.

page 51

One-fourth of the water would be left.

pages 52–53
Lizard number 1 cannot win because it is impossible to roll a 1 with two dice. The lizards that win most often will be 6, 7, and 8 because there are so many combinations of the dice that yield those numbers.

page 54
The missing number is 3.

page 55
The missing number is 2.

page 56

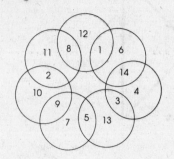

page 57
Answers will vary.

page 58
Some possible counting methods are: Cosmos can simply count his Smelly Jellies. He can count by 2s or 5s. He can count the number of Smelly Jellies in one inch of the jar, then multiply by the number of inches in the jar. He can divide the Smelly Jellies into two or more piles, then count one pile and multilpy by the number of piles.
Parent: Accept any reasonable response. Encourage original thinking.

page 59
Answers will vary. Many combinations of scores are possible.

page 60

Mack	7	licorice
Flack	8	popcorn
Jack	6	chocolate bars